The Speed Trap Bible:

How to Successfully Handle Your Traffic Ticket

By: Robert W. Rushing, Jr.

William Wilberforce Press

2014

Unless your foot is lighter than a twig, it's happened to you. You knew the reputation of the town. You saw the intricately carved sign at the city limits, welcoming you to wherever it was you happened to be. You might have noticed the smaller sign posted inconspicuously nearby, in the shade of a tall tree or otherwise obscured. It advised you of an abrupt drop in the legal speed limit.

Or maybe you missed it. It's easy to do, what with Bluetooth, satellite radio, and all the other bells and whistles on a modern automobile. Regardless, you certainly didn't miss the siren and the blue light, or the humorless, uniformed officer as he approached your vehicle.

If it seems as if there's more to this than a concern for highway safety, you're correct. In these hard economic times, everyone is looking for an easy way to make a buck. Cities and municipalities are no exception. In the past several years, the number of speeding tickets written to motorist has skyrocketed, as have the amount of the fines. This is no coincidence. It improves the bottom line, and because it theoretically punishes a wrongdoer, it goes down easier with the local citizenry than a tax increase.

By virtue of being on the road, you become a target. Furthermore, while few are willing to admit it, certain factors make you more likely to get a ticket. For example, if you have an out of state license plate, it stands to reason that you will probably just put a check in the mail and never be heard from again. Since trials are expensive, this is good for the bottom line.

If you are traveling late at night, you are also more at risk. This mostly has to do with the amount of traffic on the road. If you are one of six speeders traveling in close proximity on a stretch of road, the numbers favor you, because like a jungle predator, the cop must single out one from the herd. Ironically, as in nature, the unlucky victim is usually the slowest of the group.

The type of car you drive can also be a factor. Sports cars, or any vehicle known to be designed for speed, will get the attention not only of the girl of your dreams, but attract cops like bees to honey. So can something as seemingly insignificant as a bumper sticker. I once gave a friend one that said "
Never drink and drive. You might hit a bump and spill your drink." She was actually going to put it on her car. I stopped her.

Or you might just be pulled because the officer has nothing better to do, and sees an easy opportunity to write up a minor violation. For example, in the past few years, most states have passed mandatory seatbelt laws. In my home state, this went on the books with lukewarm support, much hoopla, and assurances that a violation of the seatbelt law alone would not be a legal basis for a highway stop.

Of course, politicians being what they are, the law was amended a few months later during the Christmas holidays, to allow for highway stops. Now we have a new holiday tradition: ads featuring large numbers of sunglasses wearing, uniformed cops surrounded by squad cars, to an ominous soundtrack reminding you that "they are watching." They do not lie. I have had two tickets myself for not wearing the harness, which causes me shoulder pain.

My point? Simply that there are many reasons why you might get pulled and ticketed. Some are fair. Some most definitely are not fair. Either way, one thing is certain. The minute you are pulled over by a police officer and effectively placed under arrest, you are in danger.

By saying that, I mean no disrespect to law enforcement. The truth is, there are a lot of brave and ethical people in the field, who do what they do to protect the general public. Without them, our society would be in a state of chaos and collapse. Nevertheless, what I say is exactly true.

There are several reasons for this. One of the first and foremost reasons is the fact that the police officer is operating in a state of fear. This may not be apparent, but consider the circumstances from his or her point of view.

This person is approaching a stranger, whose body, and most importantly, hands and arms, are probably out of view. He is aware that the stranger in the vehicle is in a state of agitation, fear, or both. How the person will react to the confrontation is unpredictable at best, especially if the driver is guilty of crimes other than traffic offenses. He is aware that countless of his fellow officers have been killed or seriously injured in similar situations.

As the saying goes, a caged animal is a dangerous animal. This is especially true here, where the animal in question is armed to the teeth, and has legal authority to commit acts of violence on the public.

CHAPTER ONE: HANDLING THE TRAFFIC STOP

Thus, rule one of a traffic stop is SURVIVE THE TRAFFIC STOP. However hot headed you may be, and however much you may feel that your rights have been violated, be aware of your situation. Before you open your mouth, remember the following things:

1. The arresting officer has made a judgment call to stop your vehicle. Attacking his decision to do so, or worse, hurling insults, will make things worse. To have any chance of talking yourself out of the ticket, it is essential to establish mutual respect with the officer.
2. The arresting officer is, as we have said, heavily armed and trained to protect himself. He does not know if you are a threat, and is trained to assume that you are. This means that you are in danger of serous physical injury or even death.
3. Still more to the point, you do not know how willing or anxious he might be to use his weapons and training. I have spoken to police officers who insist that a Taser is not a dangerous instrument, and that they will eagerly Taser any individual who verbally challenges them during a stop. There is a real risk to this confrontation.
4. Finally, if you are receiving a ticket, keep this in mind. If you intend to contest the ticket in court, the key witness against you will be the arresting officer. Depending on the court calendar in your jurisdiction, it will be weeks, months, or even years before the case is called to trial. During that time, the arresting officer will be involved in countless more traffic stops. You do not want to be the loudmouth jerk that made an impression on him. You want to be the routine subject that fades quickly from memory.

    For that reason, ALWAYS do the following during a traffic stop:
    1. Pull over as soon as it is clear that the officer wants you to. If it is not possible to do this immediately in safe fashion, slow down. Head immediately to a safe spot, use your turn signal as you turn off the road, and stop. Do not pull into the center divider section of the road. This is a hazard to you, the officer, and everyone else on the road.

2. As the officer approaches, keep both hands in clear view. Do not open the car door or exit the vehicle. Roll down the window.
3. Keep your cool and speak calmly. Use respectful terms when speaking to the officer. Avoid making any comment that amount to an admission of guilt. These could be used against you in court. Never say "You can't write me a ticket. I haven't done anything wrong." The officer will take this as a challenge, and go for the ticket book.
4. If possible, get your driver's license and registration out. You want to avoid having to fumble through the glove compartment or search the rest of the car with the officer standing by. This can lead to all kinds of problems.

    While we're on that subject, here's a helpful hint. If you have a smart phone, take a picture of your proof of insurance, vehicle registration and license. It is a lot easier to access the photograph on your phone under pressure than to tear through your glove compartment looking.
5. Do not hand the officer your wallet. He does not want to be accused of stealing your money, and in some jurisdictions, you don't want to give him the chance.
6. Do not argue with the officer. However, and this is crucial, it might be permissible to discuss and explain the situation. The difference is a matter of common sense, which you should be using at all times.
7. Although it should be obvious, do not ask the officer to cut you a break because you are worried about losing your license. You would think that saying "I can't get another ticket or I'll lose my license," would be the last approach you would try, even in the heat of the moment. Still, people do this all the time.

8. Especially at first, when speaking with the officer, make your comments short and responsive. "Do you know how fast you were going?" for example, would be responded to with "No sir, officer."

    If you were to respond by admitting that you were speeding, case over and negotiation leverage lost. On the other hand, if you instead responded with an answer the officer considered dishonest, things might get worse for you. Do not fall into this trap.

    For the same reasons, you should generally avoid small talk with the officer. During a traffic stop, saying the wrong thing can result in a search of your vehicle, your vehicle being towed, or a night in the cooler.

    There's an old joke about a guy who gets stopped for speeding in a small town. The officer asks him if he can see his license. The guy says "Sure, if I can play with your gun." He closes by mentioning that the town jail had the best corn bread he had ever tasted.

9. Do not cry. I debated this one back and forth. I've never spoken to an officer who would admit to being manipulated by this sort of thing. Still, you cannot discount all of the stories of women crying their way out of tickets. It can backfire if the performance comes across as fake, so better not to try unless you genuinely lose control or you are a talented actor able to perform well under pressure.
10. Do not tell the officer that you will "see him in court." This is one of those situations in which you are harming yourself by declaring your intentions. Knowing this, the officer will be sure to make careful notes about your incident, so he will be ready to testify if you are good to your word.

11. Do not beg. It works no better in this situation than in relationships.
12. Do not try to get out of the ticket with name dropping or suggesting that you have "connections." If you actually do have them, the best strategy would be to go through the process calmly and inoffensively, and involve the "connection" later. This can actually backfire if the officer decides to check around and see if the person whose name you dropped actually does know you.
13. Do not refuse to sign the ticket. Your signature is only a promise to appear in court and not an admission of guilt.

With the ground rules established, we can now discuss when and how you might attempt to talk your way out of the ticket. I hope the previous list has made it clear that the first objective here is to do no harm. If the traffic stop concludes without you having made any real impression on the officer, that in itself is a kind of success. However, if you aim for more, these things just might work:

1. If you have a real emergency, explain this. What qualifies should be obvious: having a baby (you or your significant other, right now), or health issue (you or significant other, right now) or death. Late for a court hearing has been a winner for me, but don't even try if the hearing relates to a traffic offense. I once had a client tell me that an officer let him off the hook because he was racing to make a payment to his loan shark (not confirmed.)

The point is, the excuse has to be something that would make a reasonable person disregard the traffic laws. It is also worth noting that if the excuse is good enough and original enough, the officer might just take the time to verify its truth. You do not want to run the risk of a creative lie.

2. If you genuinely believe you were driving within the speed limit, there is nothing wrong with arguing you case. Just don't lose your cool There are a few things that can commonly lead to a miscarriage of justice, for example:
   a. You are traveling on a crowded highway in a tight group of cars. In this situation, it might well be that the radar hit some other vehicle.
   b. Your speed was measured just prior to or before you entered the new speed zone. The abrupt ten, twenty, or thirty mile drop offs you find at so many town limits are not a coincidence. They are a principle source of revenue for the town. However, the question of guilt or innocence may ride on less yardage than you would need to get a first down in a football game. Take note of your surroundings, and raise the issue if appropriate.
   c. If all else fails, try sincerity. If you know you were speeding, and you were caught dead to center, admit it. A cynical policeman can be totally disarmed by a motorist who says, essentially: "I know I

was speeding and that was wrong, but officer, I have an excellent driving record. I have had a difficult day, and I am very tired. If you would see yourself clear to overlook my mistake this one time, I give you my word that you will not have to pull me over again."

d. DO NOT just make something up. Within a few months, any officer has a strong sense on when he or she is being fed a line. At best, it motivates the officer to follow up, issue you the ticket, and see to it that there is a conviction.

At the worse, it will cause him or her to view you suspiciously, which can lead to all kinds of bad consequences. While examples are too numerous to list, here are a few excuses that usually go down with a thud:

1. My speedometer is broken. I don't know how fast I'm going.
2. My cruise control is broken. I couldn't control the vehicle.
3. I am late for work, and the boss said he'd fire me if I was late one more time. (This is unlikely to work even if true.)
4. I just noticed that my tags have expired, and I was rushing to the DMV to take care of it. (Sounds good initially because it makes you sound marginally responsible. But even if true, you are essentially saying "I'm breaking the law because I realized

that I was breaking the law. So you should excuse me.)
5. I am trying to get to (fill in the blank) before it closes. (This is not likely to help, unless the place in question is a pharmacy or otherwise health care related, and the situation is truly urgent. (Filling mom's nitro glycerin prescription might qualify. Her prescription for dry eyes probably won't.)

If the officer appears interested, let him or her follow up with questions. This is a dance in which you do not want to lead. Remember, offering information can lead to new suspicions, searches of your person or vehicle, and additional charges. Answer any questions honestly and briefly, taking time to think your answers through. Anything you say at this time could end up in an incident report, or the officer's notes, and be thrown back in your face at trial. Try to steer the conversation on a narrow course of whether or not you were speeding.

The exception to this would be the situation in which the officer begins to talk about a subject completely unrelated to charging you with a crime. If you were to hear something like "Hey, isn't your son on the jayvee football team with my kid?" go with that. This might be your lucky day.

It is also important to know what represents the end game. When the officer takes out a ticket book, and begins to write, it is inevitable. You are going to get a ticket. Quietly sign the ticket. The officer will explain your obligation to appear at trial and the nature of the charge. Listen carefully. While nobody expects you to be happy at this point, try to end with a civil "Good afternoon," or something of that nature.

CHAPTER TWO: EXAMINING THE TRAFFIC TICKET

Once you drive off with ticket, it can be hard to figure out what to do. The actual piece of paper is an unwanted reminder of a negative experience, but also an important document. Too often, it ends up in the glove compartment or the console of the car, crumbled and abused, a focus for pent up hostility.

That's too bad, because it contains much essential information, and losing it can have serious consequences. For that reason, I advise people to take the simple step of either scanning a copy into the hard drive of their computer, or making several copies to keep in a safe place.

At the least, before you ball it up and use it for a basketball, make sure you document this important information elsewhere.

1. Name of arresting officer. If you are to go to trial, you need to know the name and badge number of the arresting officer. You may want to investigate his background and reputation; more on that later.
2. Name of trial judge: Again, if you are going to trial, you need to know who is going to be presiding. In small towns, there are usually only one of two judges that handle the load. In order to have the job in the first place, each will be well connected in local politics, and therefore have what can be described as a cozy relationship with local law enforcement. While- and this is crucial-there are exceptions, you can expect a heavy bias towards conviction.

As a general rule, I find that the longer the judge has served, the more likely this is to be true. I also find that a full time city or municipal judge tends to be more committed to accommodating the powers that be. However, these are generalities which might or might not apply to your situation.

If you intend to go to trial, you will want to find out more about the presiding judge. That will be discussed more fully in the next chapter.

c. The date and time of arrest. This can be important for any number of reasons. Most commonly, you might want to document the weather conditions at the time you were pulled over.

d. The date and time of trial: It is amazing just how many people fail to show up for their court date on a ticket. The result is inevitable, conviction, maximum fine and full penalty under law. Even if the driver is guilty of the charge, there is almost always an opportunity to negotiate a reduction in the sentence, saving hundreds in fines and possibly thousands by way of increased insurance costs.

You might assume that you would never forget the date and time of such an important event, especially if you have never been to court before. Time, however, dims memories and changes priorities. The first chance you get, take whatever kind of calendar you keep, and a red sharpie pen or other bold colored marker. Circle not only the date of trial, but also place reminders in bold red ink at the day twenty days prior to trial, fifteen days prior to trial, and one week prior to trial.

e. The uniform warrant number. Though procedures vary from state to state, it is essential to have the information necessary to insure that your communications with the court are linked to the right case file.

The local clerk of court, and his often underpaid or undertrained staff, might or might not be reliable. Regardless, if they make a crucial mistake in documenting your file-such as losing a request for a jury trial, or sending your notice of appearance to the wrong address, they will do everything possible to hold you responsible for the consequences. The only way to avoid this is to do everything perfectly. Hence, you always include the uniform warrant number and date of offense in every communication with the court.

f. The exact name and statute or ordinance number of the offense with which you are charged. If you plan to go to trial, you will want to check out the exact language of the law you are accused of violating. The statute can contain important information about the standard of proof required for a conviction, among other things. It will also inform you of the legal consequences of a conviction, crucial information if you wish to negotiate a settlement.

Once you have all of this information carefully recorded, you are at least in a position to make sound decisions about your case, and act on them as necessary.

CHAPTER THREE: TRIAL OR NO TRIAL?

The initial decision of what to do with the ticket is easy, becoming more complicated further on down the road.

At first, you will always want to request a jury trial. There is a simple reason for this, which is obvious if you think of the local court as what it essentially is, a business. Just like a private company, the motivation is to turn a profit which can be used to fund its future activities, or even better, fund other projects.

This is best done by moving the merchandise quickly and inexpensively. If this case, the merchandise is the traffic ticket which you "purchase" by paying the fine to generate profit.

From the perspective of local government, the best case scenario is that you would just send in a check a few days following the traffic stop. All activity beyond this cuts into profit, by adding in overhead costs such as employee time, use of court facilities, and use of officer resources.

For this reason, you have negotiation leverage even if you are actually guilty of the offense. That is, provided that you have not made the case a personal with the arresting officer by making your behavior an issue.

The ability of the court system to move cases with any kind of efficiently is conditional on having very few trials, and a large number of plea bargains. This is true not only in traffic court, but also in every other kind of criminal court system.

As such, you benefit by at least initially requesting a jury trial. It is important to understand that making this request does not mean that you are necessarily going to try the case before a jury, or at all. It simply means that you are keeping your options open.

There are a couple of important exceptions to this rule. The first relates to the situation in which you reside a long distance from the place in which you received the ticket. If this is the case, you must seriously consider whether you are willing to invest the time and expense of making one or several trips back to deal with the problem. Chances are that your lost wages and travel costs will be considerably more than the amount of the fine, something the court and local law enforcement are aware of and rely on.

For years, I lived in a town about two hours away from a major resort area. There was no interstate access, so the roads traveled by vacationers passed through several small towns. Each had one or several traffic cops, hidden behind large billboards welcoming tourists to town to shop or dine. The intent was clearly to collect revenue, one way or the other.

I would regularly get the call from a tourist who had returned home and forgot about the ticket until shortly prior to or worse, after the date of trial. Absent unusual circumstances, actually pulling a jury and trying the case was not an option, although it was still possible to get a good result.

The other special circumstance involves the case where there is more at stake than would initially appear. In some situations, an individual simply cannot afford the consequences of a conviction on the offense with which he or she has been charged.

For example, if you are a trucker, a ticket might result in loss of your job, or suspension of your commercial driver's license. If you already have a number of points on your license, it might be that if you are convicted the penalty for this particular ticket will be loss of your job.

If this is the case, attempt to resolve the case quickly in a way that avoids the worst possible result. You do not want to assume the risk of missing a trial date, with all of the harsh consequences.

Since the court wants to discourage jury trials, many intentionally make it as difficult for possible for those who desire one. For example, some municipalities require numerous court appearances, often of negligible importance or virtually pointless, requiring the appearance of both the accused and his or her legal counsel.

From their perspective, this has the additional benefit of increasing the cost of legal representation, again making it easier to convict.

Failure to appear for a pretrial hearing, mediation or for the qualification of a jury can result in a conviction, even though nothing is accomplished that could not have been handled through the mail or otherwise.

My point is that the process can be intentionally unfair, and often is. If you are determined to bring your case to trial, you must be aware of this. The pending court case will have to be a priority. You must be willing to drop almost anything else going on in your life to attend to this business on relatively short notice.

I have enclosed two versions of the letter I send requesting a jury trial in a traffic ticket case. The first version is for use in a case in which the hope is to negotiate a settlement prior to trial and is attached as Exhibit A in the appendix of the book. The second version is for use in a case expected to go to trial, and is enclosed as Exhibit B in the appendix of the book.

Whichever one you choose to send, always follow these rules.

1. Send the letter at least ten days prior to the court hearing. Remember, if the court does not get the letter in time, you will be found guilty. It will be your problem, and an uphill struggle, to prove that you acted appropriately to invoke your right to a trial.

2. Always send at least one copy of the letter by certified mail, return receipt requested. This is the only way to get written proof that you requested a jury trial. Keep the proof of mailing and a copy of the letter together in a safe place. When you get the receipt, put it in the file with the rest.

3. Make sure that you specifically request a trial by jury. Unless the judge is your golfing buddy, the golfing buddy of your lawyer, etc. assume that the relationship between the local judge and local law enforcement creates inevitable bias towards conviction.

    Who do you expect the judge to believe, a stranger traveling through town or an officer who has appeared in his courtroom possibly hundreds of times?

4. Put careful thought as to the reply address used in the letter. City courts are notorious for providing short or totally inadequate notice to defendants in traffic court.

 I have heard stories from clients about leaving town for the weekend, or a matter of days, and finding a certified notice in the mailbox. After rushing to the post office, they picked up a letter notifying them to be in traffic court at some pont in the recent past.

The smart money is on making a call to the local clerk of court early on in the process. Ask about how terms of court are scheduled, and how much notice is customarily given to defendants prior to the term. Also, ask if there is a municipal or state law that governs the process, and if possible, get a copy of the statute for yourself. Find out if the court publishes its roster of cases for trial on line, and if so, how to access the web site. This is the best way to avoid losing the game before it starts.

CHAPTER FOUR: NEGOTIATION

The negotiation process for a traffic ticket is relatively simple. There is only one issue to be discussed since, if you are agreed to a negotiated plea, you are conceding that you are guilty of some offense. All that remains is to work out a penalty in fines or points that is agreeable to all.

Many cities across the nation have an offense on the book that is often referred to as "careless operation of a vehicle." This is an intentionally broad, catchall term for just about anything that a police officer might observe, and use as justification for a traffic stop.

These statutes are often written explicitly for the purpose of facilitating plea negotiation. For example, in some localities, a plea to "Careless Operation" will double the amount of the fine, but result in no points which would affect the driving record of the defendant. This can prevent the otherwise inevitable and sometimes substantial increase in insurance costs which would otherwise occur.

In response to criticism from the insurance industry, new restrictions have been placed on many of these statutes. Often, the statute provides that a driver can plead to "careless operation" one time only.

It is also worth noting that over time, some of the insurance carriers have begun to access local traffic court conviction records to document these offenses. As such, before paying the additional fine, try to determine if this arrangement is actually going to provide you with any benefit.

This can be difficult. Possibly the best method is to ask anyone else you know who has pled to "careless operation of a vehicle" and had time to receive his or her next insurance bill. If not, post the question on social media, or better yet, ask an attorney or court official. Whatever response you get, evaluate it while carefully considering the source (A court official, for example, will want to "sell" the more expensive ticket. Thus, if he or she tells you that the arrangement is not likely to prevent your insurance company from increasing your premium costs, this would be highly reliable information, as it would be against his or her interest to tell you this.)

Otherwise, most traffic or municipal courts have a standard plea offer; reduce the fine by one half, or reduce the points by one half. Often, the arresting officer or prosecuting attorney will offer this as a take it or leave it deal. If this a good offer? Yes, if you are guilty of the offense.

Which option should you take? That depends on several factors. Among them are your driving record and your short term financial situation. If you already have traffic offenses on your record, you have to worry about an increase in your insurance costs. You would probably want to negotiate the points portion of the penalty down as much as possible; generally, a six point offense will reduce to three, a four to two, etc.

What if you cannot afford to pay the fine? In many situations, courts will agree to wait awhile for the money. Ask, and if you find this is a possibility, ask for more time than you think you need. Life happens, and you will not get another extension of time if you have trouble later coming up with the cash.

If there is no possibility of getting an extension of the time in which to pay, negotiate the fine down as low as possible. You can expect your fine to be an alternative to jail time, so if you do not pay, there will be consequences. Resist the temptation at this time to make a promise you cannot keep. Again, a fifty percent reduction seems to be where many draw the line in the sand. However, if you have a special hardship, it might be possible to do better.

Finally, how you pay matters. Most courts do not accept personal checks, something many will fail to mention. If possible, it is best to simply go to the court, bring cash or certified funds in the form they prefer, and make the payment in person. That way, you do not have to worry about your check being lost in the mail or misplaced by the court. You have your receipt in hand, and problem solved.

CHAPTER FIVE: TRIAL

As with any court case, more than anything, winning or losing has everything to do with preparation. There are several things you MUST DO before you go to court:

1. If possible, find out what you can about the arresting officer or officers. This can admittedly be difficult.

However, it can also be vitally important. You might, for example, find evidence of bias on the part of the officer or past misconduct.

Unfortunately, it is far more difficult to find this kind of evidence as to an individual in law enforcement than it is as to an average citizen. These are the best options:

a) If you consider it necessary, find out what state agency investigates and documents police misconduct. Contact them, preferably in some written form, and inquire as to the status of the officer. If there is an investigative file on the officer, arrange to obtain a copy of it. If necessary, issue a subpoena through the court to accomplish this, or make a request pursuant to the Freedom of Information Act.

Check him or her out on social media. People post surprising and often stupid things on the internet. Those in law enforcement are no exception.

2) Make similar inquires with regards to the presiding judge. If the judge is a member of the state bar, things get a little easier here. The Bar will advise you whether the Judge has ever been professionally disciplined, and in some states, as to whether there is a pending disciplinary action against him or her. In all probability, there will not be, but there is a chance.

Again, attempt to check out his or her reputation on social media. If nothing else, you will at least know what to expect in court.

b) Get a copy of the list of jurors as soon as possible. Once you get a notice for a court date, contact the clerk of court and ask for a copy of the list. If you have friends in the area, ask them to review the list and to have their own friends in turn review the list. You want to know as much as possible about those who will decide the issue of your guilt or innocence.

      i)   While you will get some of this information on the date of trial when the jury is "qualified", you want to get more, and get it sooner. Good things to know include marital status, work history, all group affiliations such as churches, charities, etc., political affiliation, whether the juror has children and if so, their ages.

2.   Go to the scene of the crime, and bring a camera. Chances are that if you are not familiar with the area, you have a less than perfect recollection of the place. It is important to look the area over critically, well before the date of the trial. Look closely at details such as the locations of signs and traffic signals, anything that could limit visibility for yourself or the officer (trees that obscure signs, or the line of sign of the officer as he aims the radar gun, for example), and any physical evidence which remains from the incident, such as skid marks on the road.

Take pictures from various angles, so that you can explain your story to a jury. You might also want to measure any relevant distances if this is helpful. If so, make your visit at a time when traffic is light to avoid further problems with the law.

3. If there are witnesses, get written statements from them as soon as possible. These will not be admissible in court. However, they serve two purposes. Firstly, they insure that your witness will not forget the important points of his or her testimony. Secondly, if your witness becomes uncooperative, already having a statement written in their hand makes it very difficult for them to avoid telling the truth later in court.
4. Take some time to prepare your own pre- trial notes. This is necessary to organize your thoughts, and allow you to prepare for trial. Some of the things you would want to include in your notes are:

A. Was the officer alone, or did he have a partner? If so, who was driving?
   (You might be able to find inconsistencies in their testimony at trial. Also, the driver would arguably be distracted in observing you because he was preoccupied with driving the car.)
B. What was the weather and traffic conditions like at the time? (Bad weather could affect the officer's opportunity to observe you. A large amount of traffic on the road could lead to issues about questions about the reliability of radar, among other things.)
C. Did anyone say anything to you that might lead to the conclusion that the arresting officer was biased against you for any reason? This might include the fact that you drive a "fast" car, your youth, race, or gender. If so, document this as accurately as possible.

D. What were you first told when asked why your vehicle was stopped? (If it was for some reason other than speeding, this might lead to an argument that the officer suspected something else, but wrote you up on the lesser charge when the initial suspicion proved wrong.)
E. If you have had any prior dealings with the arresting officer either professionally or personally, document these. Do they lead to any inference that he or she might have had a bias against you?
F. Was there any problem with the operation of your vehicle at the time? A defective speedometer is a rare thing on a late model car, but does happen. If this is the case, find a mechanic to repair it who will keep the defective parts and is willing to testify. Same thing with a defective cruise control, etc.
G. If there is some explanation by way of emergency for your rate of speed, document the truth of this. (ie. If you were rushing to the bed side of a dying parent, bring along the obituary. If your wife was at the hospital giving birth, bring the birth certificate and pictures of the baby, if not the *actual* baby.)
H. If there are skid marks or other physical evidence relevant to the case, photograph and take to court. In the case of skid marks, the length of the mark is crucial as this can determine the rate of speed for the vehicle. Measure carefully with a yard stick held up close to the mark in the road, and photograph. Also, be sure the photograph is dated.
I. If there is a crucial witness, urge them to attend or make them, especially if their story potentially resolves the issue of guilt or innocence. (For example, your friend was a passenger, and says "we were going to a wedding. I know he wasn't speeding because I was doing my makeup in the car and told him to go

slow.")Remember, you can issue a subpoena through the court to require a witness to attend.

J. Collect any evidence you might use to bolster your credibility in court. For example, if you wish to point out that you have a "good driver" discount from your insurance company bring the statement showing the discount. If you are a young driver, and just got an "A" in driver's education, bring your report car or even the driving instructor.

5. Review these materials, organize them, and come up with a plan. One of the most common mistakes made by non-attorneys is to simply show up for court, start talking, and hope for the best.

As in sports, success comes to those who act purposefully and are well prepared. If you were a football coach, wouldn't you carefully consider the strengths and weaknesses of your team before the game, compare them to the strengths and weaknesses of the opposition, and then decide how to give your team the best chance of winning? A trial is no different.

When you are done, you should be able to write out your theory of the case in a single sentence. By this, I mean a little more than just "I did not speed", also an explanation of why. For example:

"I did not speed because my car was overheating and I was trying to get it home without being stranded."

"I did not speed because my girlfriend and I were having an argument and about to break up. I was looking for a place to pull over."

"I did not speed because I know a lot of people get tickets at that intersection and I'm always extra careful there."

What if you have a second or even a third argument? Simply include a second or third sentence. For example:

"Also, I had broken my glasses and my vision was good enough to drive, but not the best. I had slowed down because I wasn't seeing as well." (This one could be a slippery slope that would open up a whole new can of worms.)

"Also, my girlfriend had just hit me in the head with her cell phone. I had taken

my foot off the accelerator to feel the bump on my head. (ditto)

Now what remains is to organize your testimony and exhibits for trial. Don't write out word for word what you want to say. This makes you sound wooden, contrived and insincere; all bad things with a jury. Instead, organize your thoughts as talking points that need to be mentioned.

For example, you might want to make a note to remind yourself to mention: 1. My girlfriend and I were arguing, 2. I had slowed down to listen to her, because she was saying I never listened to her. 3. She hit me in the head with her cell phone, which really hurt. 4. I took my foot completely off the accelerator and slowed down to a crawl. 5. I was never going more than (insert mph) miles per hour through that area, because I know that people get pulled there all the time.

This is a well thought out presentation, which should be believable, especially if the girlfriend (or ex-girlfriend) shows up to testify on your behalf. Of course, there might be a domestic violence charge coming to one or the other of you, but that's another book entirely.

If you have physical exhibits such as photographs, make a list of what will be presented and in what order. You would want to present these to the judge with the opposing attorney or the officer who will try the case present, and ask if there are any objections. This can prevent awkward moments in front of the jury that could make you look bad.

At the same time, you should be allowed to review any exhibits which will be presented by the arresting officer or the prosecuting attorney. If these are photographs, insist that you be provided details as to how and under what circumstances they were taken. Today, these most likely would be taken from a camera attached to the patrol vehicle.

More importantly, require the officer to provide "Chain of custody" evidence with regards to the photographs. By this, you will be insisting that the arresting officer inform you and the court of where the pictures have been stored since they were taken, and who has had access to the film or the container in which it was stored. This information is vital to insure that the film was not mislabeled, and that nothing else happened which would bring into question its authenticity.

Now, we will discuss the best possible scenario. What if you are noticed for trial, show up, and the arresting officer does not show up or better yet, quits the force before trial? Jackpot!

You move for dismissal, which should be granted. Any bail you paid at the time should be refunded, and your record is clean. Actually, it is a little known secret, but law enforcement is a career with a high rate of turn over. It is arguably worth the trouble of asking for a jury trial and running through the hoops on the chance that this will happen.

If you actually end up trying the case, here are a few tips.

1. In general, pick a jury of people who appear open minded and willing to at least consider the possibility that an authority figure could be accidentally or intentionally wrong. Unfortunately, these do not necessarily grow on trees, and don't always wear a T shirt that clues you in (although this does happen from time to time.) Experts have been analyzing the art, for it is not a science, of jury selection for years, and there is still no consensus on what works best. If all else fails, avoid the best dressed people in the room, who are probably a little too respectful of authority. Try to select people as

much like you as possible with regards to age, race, values, income, etc.

2. You will be told that the opening argument should be short and you should not argue the facts of the case. However, the opening is important. Keep it simple. Make eye contact with the jurors and introduce yourself. Tell them that you will give them a brief, honest, and clear account of what happened that day. Ask them for and thank them in advance for their attention.

This will also be a good time to establish your good citizen credentials. Mention that you that you respect the arresting officer and the service he is providing to the community. Explain that you are a law abiding citizen who respects law enforcement and the service it provides. You are contesting the ticket because you are innocent.

3. You will testify first. Again, look the jury in the eye. Go over your prepared talking points. Take your time, relax, and be clear. If you have photographs or other documents, be sure to enter them into the case as exhibits. If you are representing yourself, the trial judge will ordinarily assist you in this.

4. The prosecuting attorney or arresting officer will then have a chance to ask you questions. This is called "cross examination." He or she will be allowed to ask what are called "leading" questions, which essentially means questions that imply an answer, because you

are what is called a hostile witness. For example, you might be asked:

"You saw the big sign on the right side of the road that said "School Zone-reduce speed" didn't you?"

The idea is to get a yes or no answer, and prevent any explanation. Do not be bullied into playing that game. Listen to the question carefully, and take a moment if you need it. If you do not understand the question, ask that the question be rephrased or repeated. This is a better tactic than just sitting and looking out to space, which might give the jury the wrong idea.

If the honest answer is not an absolute yes or no, respond accordingly. You might say, for instance:

"I saw something on a post, but it was covered up by tree branches."

If you consider what the arresting officer needs to prove to convict you, you can anticipate what you will be asked on cross examination. It is important to be ready. The wrong response or looking uncomfortable can ruin your case.

The good news is, you also get a shot at this. Remember the homework you did before trial? After the officer presents his case, you will get the chance to bring out whatever you found. However, and this is crucial, keep in mind that most juries have a great deal of respect for law enforcement, and do not like people who insult or berate policemen. Unless the situation is really ugly, keep it civil and respectful. It is essential that the jury like you.

What you will most likely do on cross examination is address any inconsistencies in the testimony of the arresting officer. While he speaks, listen carefully and take notes, always looking for details in his account that are inaccurate. This can cause a jury to question whether his entire account of the event is for one reason or another inaccurate.

Remember that you will now be allowed to ask "leading" questions. To form a leading question, end the question with a phrase such as "isn't it?", "wasn't it?" or "don't they?" The purpose is to make the witness answer yes or no, as opposed to explaining the answer. For example:

"That tree branch completely covers the school zone sign except for the bottom of the post, doesn't it?"

"There is no way a driver approaching from that intersection could see that it was a school zone sign, could they?"

If the officer attempts to deny, you would have photographs of the obscured sign ready for the jury. If he attempts to explain his answer, ask the judge to remind him that this is cross examination, and all you require is a simple yes or no answer.

If there are additional witnesses, the process would be the same. The party who called the witness to court would question them first, and then the opposition would cross examine them.

5. The case concludes with the closing argument. As the defendant, you get to make the initial closing argument, and also a reply to the closing presented by the arresting officer or prosecuting attorney.

This is the stage in the trial at which you can show off your acting chops. Review your notes before you begin, and make sure to remind the jury of the important points you raised in your testimony. If you have an argument as to why the arresting officer is incorrect or inaccurate as to the facts of the case, now is the time to explain it to the jury. For example:

"The city has left those tree branches uncut for years, even though every other tree and shrub within five hundred yards of the school is neatly trimmed. Whether this is intentional or not, it keeps anyone who is not from this town from seeing the school zone sign, slowing down, and not getting a ticket. I should not be convicted for failing to obey a sign that is completely hidden."

Be a responsible editor, and limit the number of points you make in your closing argument. Remember that the more you talk the less of it that will register with the jury. Emphasize the key points. Also, remember the principle of primacy and recency. People tend to remember what you say first and what you say last, the middle not so much.

At this point, the case is turned over to the jury. The Judge will engage in a process referred to as "charging" a jury. This is essentially advising the jurors of the law and statutes applicable to the case. You will have an opportunity to review the materials and should review these materials carefully. Usually, however, the charge is not a controversial issue.

From there, you are waiting for the jury to return. In traffic court, where consequences are not so severe, the wait is usually no more than an hour. If you win, Congratulations! Anyone who successfully takes on any level of governmental authority and comes out ahead should be proud. If not, you do have the right to appeal. Time limits vary from state to state but are uniformly brief, so act quickly if you are so inclined.

CHAPTER SIX: DO YOU NEED A LAWYER?

There are good reasons to consider hiring a lawyer to handle this kind of matter for you. Pretty clearly, your chance of a positive outcome increases when you add an experienced professional to your team. Not only will your presentation appear more polished and persuasive to a jury, but your decision making will be in all likelihood be stronger.

The real question is whether your exposure in fines and increased insurance costs justifies the expense. If you have not had a ticket in years, the answer is probably no. This is especially true if your insurance has an accident forgiveness clause, which will allow you one violation without an increase in your premiums.

However, if you have multiple violations, and are at risk of losing your license, you need to invest in an attorney. The investment will likely be returned many times over in reduced insurance costs. I can say this without even considering the other serious financial consequences of losing your transportation.

Likewise, if you possess a commercial driver's license, and operate a vehicle for a living, it is wise to treat all moving violations with great care. Due to the amount of time you are on the road, it is possible to accumulate violations in bunches, and suddenly find your livelihood at risk. The points you surrendered without a fight might suddenly come back to haunt you.

Of course, if you are charged with something more serious than speeding, such as an alcohol related offense, the question is a no brainer. The laws related to driving while impaired are harsh without exception, and a single violation is life changing. This sort of situation must be handled with the utmost care and professionalism.

So how do you choose an attorney? Finding a lawyer who will represent you in traffic court is never a problem. Try any search engine, or do it the old fashioned way and check the yellow pages. You will find several competing for your business, even if you are in a small town.

The problem is how to get quality at a cost effective price. A splashy ad on the internet proves nothing but that the law firm in question understands something about marketing. An unrealistically low quote to handle the matter might be nothing more than a bait and switch tactic, which does not suggest that the lawyer in question deserves your trust.

The best way to find an attorney, or any other kind of service for that matter, is to ask around. Talk to friends who have been in the same situation, and ask them whether they hired a lawyer, and if they were satisfied. A "yes" from a person you trust is probably the best indication that you are making a wise choice.

If possible, it is a good idea to consult at least two attorneys before hiring one. Unlike doctors, the effectiveness of an attorney depends to a great deal on his or her relationship with the client. A lawyer can be highly skilled and diligent, but incompatible with another personality. This will not make for a good working relationship, or a good result in court. Since moving violations are generally on the cheaper end of the legal services spectrum, you can arrange at least a couple of consultations at relatively low cost.

It is always a good idea to perform your due diligence before hiring. Go to the state bar web site, and check the name of the attorney in question. This way, before money changes hands, you can find out about any former or pending ethical violations; better safe than sorry.

Always carefully review your retainer agreement. On a case of this sort, it is best to negotiate a flat fee agreement. In other words, to pay a set amount of money for the service of representing you with regards to the ticket.

Paying an attorney by the hour can get expensive very quickly. In a case in which your typical financial exposure is a fine of less than a thousand dollars, you could run the risk of incurring far more expense in legal costs. Insist on a written retainer agreement. Never hire a lawyer without one.

Also, make sure that the contract specifies exactly what you are paying for. Just specifying the amount, without describing the services, provides no protection at all. The agreement should specify that the retainer is for services up to and including trial of the case. Accept nothing else. However, it is worth noting that almost without exception, the agreement will not require the attorney to file an appeal for you.

If possible, hire an attorney who lives and works in the area in which you got the ticket. This is an area of the law in which connections are important. An super lawyer from out of town might not serve you as well as a mediocre one who went to high school with the arresting officer and presiding judge. In a perfect world, such things would be irrelevant. The world is anything but.

If you are clueless as to where to find such a person, ask a friend who lives in the area, or if all else fails, ask the clerk of court for a traffic court roster. Find the two or three attorneys who are handling the majority of the cases, and call one of two of them. This should get you to somebody highly comfortable with the other players you have to deal with.

Keep in mind that lawyers charge for their time, and if you convince the attorney that you won't take much of it, the price can be negotiated downwards. For this reason, if you really have no intention or desire to try the case before a jury, be up front about this. The attorney will most likely offer you a substantially reduced price to negotiate a plea bargain. You will get what you need, and avoid paying for what you don't.

CONCLUSION

Sooner or later, almost everybody gets ticketed for a moving violation. While a traffic offense, unless it is alcohol or drug related, is generally not considered a serious crime, there are serious consequences when a conviction results. These include, but are not limited to, fines and other costs.

For this reason, it is almost always a mistake to simply write a check and send it in. This benefits the system, but might result in serious consequences for you. You always get something worthwhile if you prolong the case and give the impression that you might not go away quietly.

Early on, decide for yourself whether you are seeking to prove your innocence and intend to take the case to trial, or simply seeking to negotiate the best possible deal. You cannot make intelligent choices through the process without making this determination first. Then consider whether or not you wish to retain an attorney. If so, the sooner that attorney is hired, the more time he or she will have to prepare your case.

Keep in mind that, particularly in smaller towns, one speeding ticket can quickly become several. Once a vehicle is familiar to local law enforcement, and officers are watching it, more tickets are likely. If your problem occurred in an municipality you can avoid returning to, this might be a good choice, particularly if your case goes to trial.

APPENDIX

1. Request for Jury Trial Form Letter A.
2. Request for Jury Trial Form Letter B.

FORM A.

January 09, 2014

Central Traffic Court

(Address)

Re: Uniform Warrant Number: D 000921

Date of Incident: January 4, 2014

Charge: Speeding 65/55
CERTIFIED MAIL

Dear Sirs:

Please take this as my request for a trial by jury in the above referenced matter. Please forward all future correspondence in this matter to me at (insert most reliable mailing address), or alternately, contact me at (e mail address) or (telephone number.)

Respectfully,

FORM B

January 9, 2014

Central Traffic Court

(insert address)
CERTIFIED MAIL

Uniform Warrant Number: D 000921

Date of Incident: January 4, 2014

Charge: 65/55

Dear Sirs:

    Please take this as notice of my request for a trial by jury in the above referenced matter. Please forward all future correspondence to me at (home address). I can alternately be contacted at (e mail address) or reached by telephone at (include number and second reliable number if applicable).

I would appreciate the opportunity to discuss the possible resolution of this matter on mutually agreeable terms prior to trial if possible.

Respectfully,

www.ingramcontent.com/pod-product-compliance
Lightning Source LLC
Chambersburg PA
CBHW051823170526
45167CB00005B/2136